T0149256

INSPIRING GRACE

as an Alpha-holic

LINDY LEWIS

BALBOA.
PRESS

A DIVISION OF HAY HOUSE

Cover Design: Emerald Dumas
Book Design: Emerald Dumas
Photographs: Marie-Dominique Verdier

Jewelchic Jewelry Design, thank you
Meagan for my happy necklace!

Balboa Press books may be ordered through booksellers or by contacting:

Balboa Press
A Division of Hay House
1663 Liberty Drive
Bloomington, IN 47403
www.balboapress.com
1 (877) 407-4847

Because of the dynamic nature of the Internet, any web addresses or
links contained in this book may have changed since publication and
may no longer be valid. The views expressed in this work are solely those
of the author and do not necessarily reflect the views of the publisher,
and the publisher hereby disclaims any responsibility for them.

The author of this book does not dispense medical advice or prescribe the use
of any technique as a form of treatment for physical, emotional, or medical
problems without the advice of a physician, either directly or indirectly. The
intent of the author is only to offer information of a general nature to help
you in your quest for emotional and spiritual well-being. In the event you use
any of the information in this book for yourself, which is your constitutional
right, the author and the publisher assume no responsibility for your actions.

Any people depicted in stock imagery provided by Thinkstock are models,
and such images are being used for illustrative purposes only.
Certain stock imagery © Thinkstock.

Print information available on the last page.

ISBN:978-1-5043-8182-6 (sc)
ISBN: 978-1-5043-8211-3 (e)

Library of Congress Control Number: 2017908936

Balboa Press rev. date: 08/31/2017

"INSPIRATIONAL! Love the helpful reminders and how-to's of moving softly into Grace with ease, love and acceptance. Lindy has provided us Type "A"s with another reminder to accept ourselves "Quirks and all" unconditionally, to embrace ours and other's "You-niqueness" and to honor the "pause". Being Zentered is my new favorite way of being! Enjoying the "Magic in the moment" and on a "Love Loop" high!"

- Christine Schader
Certified Financial Planner

ANOTHER NIP & TUCK FOR WEBSTER

LINDY'S LANGUAGE:

80HD: The way my son heard his ADHD diagnosis; now a reminder that each beautiful brain interprets so YOU-niquely.

Alpha-demic: A woman who has thrown herself into her schooling, with the goals of external validation and good grades; potentially overshadowing the joy of learning and the value of knowledge gained.

Alpha-fall: Frequent relapses where one forgets to stay in the flow and present; lets self doubt creep in, and generally 'gets stuck in the muck.'

Alpha-holic: We are who we are, it is our innate personality, this over-acheiving, solution driven, multitasking personality. It's a beauty but she needs to be softened, with energy on purpose.

Alpha Overdrive: The natural 'Type A' speed; steamrolling ahead with no real regard for opinions or reflections; usually exhausting herself.

Black Sheep: Previously considered a misfit or viewed in a negative light, the RAF owns and embraces those things that differentiate her from her family, colleagues, or peers.

Expectations: Resentment in the making.

Faith-forward: Trusting your knowing; choosing to move fearlessly in the direction that inherently calls on a gut level; dharma.

Flow: A beautiful experience when one is so engaged in something fulfilling that it seems to literally flow from a higher plane.

JOMO: Joy of Missing Out.

Magik: Magik in the moment; embracing what's to come instead of fearing it; in this place of unknown is where the magik happens.

Momentfulness: Being really present, aware, and engaged only in what is happening to the point that distractions hold no power; leaving one clear and focused.

Munay: Nourishing, all-encompassing love.

Pause: Space; the pause has great power.

Quirks: Colors or peculiar behavioral habits that comprise aspects of that individual's character and personality.

RAF (Recovering Alpha Female): One who chooses to soften and allow her beautiful feminine spirit to unfold, transform, and inspire.

Smile: A glow of Grace upon one's face.

Stuff: Not only physical belongings, but also the thoughts, emotions, values, and expectations one holds.

Volun-tell, Volun-told: When one person "volunteers" another for a job, task, or to do something; forcing involvement without asking.

Zenter: A blended word combining Zen and center, a place of quiet to plug into intuition and trust.

So many Woo-Woo Gurus have been pivotal to my journey of moving into Grace. I have partnered with Western, Eastern, and everything-in-between healers. These gurus are Berta Kuhnel, Colleen Russell, Dauray Tannahill, Dr. Louisa Lavy, Elysabeth Williamson, Joan Jackson, Julie Hutslar, Leslie Villeli, Lisa Scoffield, Nicole Hutto, Optimum Health Institute, Peter Mico, Shannon Foley, and Sohini Huguenin.

My Woo-Woo Gurus list wouldn't be complete without including the wonderful Youngers who have held space as I've grown, transformed, and come to recognize that Grace is not just a prayer, but a lifestyle. Cia Hanford inspires me by living her truth with her You-nique free spirit, John Hanford has been my teacher of unconditional acceptance, and Jerry Hanford who continues to hold that grounded, optimal omega energy for me.

These Woo-Woo Gurus have become my tribe. They hold space and even celebrate my loving spirit as I continue to live in my authenticity and fluidity. Through this Walk of Grace, I have come to realize I must also be my own Woo-Woo Guru, utilizing what I have learned from the members of my tribe. As I become wiser and start to love, accept, and trust myself more, I continue to develop a strong sense of gratitude for my role on this planet.

There is one other encouraging group of colorful personalities that I would like to address. Emerald Dumas, Kate Lyster, Scout Anatricia, Trish Stockton, and Lorna Brewer are the women who embolden me every day to stay in my Walk. They are my team; my editors, collaborators, promoter, checkbook balancer, graphic designer, and believers in the movement.

This cultivation of gratitude toward myself, along with my tribe, Youngers, and team has inspired me to find gratitude for everyone that I can learn from. I find a little Woo-Woo Guru in everyone as they, too, help to guide my journey. I would also love to share my gratitude for my family who offer their generous, loving support all-ways!

Munay ♡ Lindy

WHAT LIES WITHIN

The Journey Continues:

THE ALPHA EPIDEMIC

HELLO, MY NAME IS LINDY, AND I AM AN ALPHA-HOLIC. The title of the first book in this trilogy utilized the word "recover*ing*" for a very good reason, as even now I realize that I am definitely not recovered.

So, welcome to the second volume of what is absolutely NOT a series of self-help books. Sure, you might have found it in the self-help section, but it's so much less about learning a whole bunch of new things and so much more about accepting what you already know and are. In my opinion, self-help books can illuminate your deficits to make you feel like you are more messed up than you really are, like you are not enough and are in need of fixing, and that's simply just not true. You are YOU-nique, and this is a chance to recognize and cultivate that in and for yourself.

If you've read the previous volume, *Recovering Alpha Female,* then you likely have an idea of what to expect from the layout and content of this book. While the goal is certainly to offer what is needed, keep those expectations in check. As I like to say, **Expectation is Resentment in the Making!** Instead of believing that you know exactly what you're going to get out of these pages, keep an open mind and let the words have their own space to whisper to you and provide the meaning you need, rather than the one you expect. Grab a cup of tea, uncap your highlighter, or maybe lay out your "happy pens" and continue to enjoy the journey.

INSTEAD OF BELIEVING THAT YOU KNOW EXACTLY WHAT YOU'RE GOING TO GET OUT OF THESE PAGES, KEEP AN OPEN MIND AND LET THE WORDS HAVE THEIR OWN SPACE

I was (eventually) able to let go of many of my **expectations** while writing this book, and it has had an authentic influence on the outcome. As many authors will tell you, creating a book is very much like birthing a child. And, like pregnancy and birth, the second "child" is just not quite as scary as the first. I hadn't counted on this or even realized it was going to happen, but I sure am glad I didn't stick with my **expectation** that it was going to be a terrifyingly difficult process. It reminds me that recovering from my Alpha ways is a daily practice and that the more open I am to it, the more I see **Grace** in my life. My Alpha side still rears its head from time to time. After all, being an Alpha Female is a huge part of my personality. It's been my go-to and comfort zone for many years.

Recognizing, accepting, and **holding space** for myself has required a beautiful and much-needed transition. Sometimes embracing this aspect of who I am is a pretty good thing, but it can also feel like a relapse. When it comes to making these kinds of major changes, it's important to remember that we are recovering, not "recovered."

CHOOSING THE
CHECKLIST

**I KNOW THAT IN THE LAST BOOK I TOLD YOU
TO CHUCK THE CHECKLIST, BUT NOW THAT
YOU'RE A LITTLE WISER, I THINK YOU'RE
READY FOR IT.** So, the checklist is back, but this time
it is authentic, nurturing, and graceful.

The amped and ramped, racked and stacked, instant-
gratification characteristics of our culture are total
energy suckers. It isn't exactly a nurturing or graceful
world out there right now. We have the kids, the cars,
the hairstyles, the appointments, the neighbors, and
so much more. It's a list that is impossible to juggle
without having our light and energy sucked right out of
us. We are at a time where it is more critical than ever
to learn how to manage our own energies. Find a **Woo-
Woo Guru,** establish your tribe, and replenish your
energy. One way that I have found useful for managing
my energy is by **Choosing the Checklist.** This is my
self-care, self-compassion, energy-restoring checklist
that helps me to get through the day or the month. The
checklist has no time limit, and, like everything else,

must be used in balance to ensure positive results. Your checklist will probably look different than mine, but here are some examples to get you started.

- Get a massage
- Take a hot bath
- Grab coffee with a girlfriend
- Update your hairstyle
- Get some acupuncture therapy
- Participate in the Love Loop
- Go somewhere that you feel Zentered
- Soak your feet at home and watch a chick flick
- Get a numerology reading
- Take pictures outside
- Do something you enjoyed when you were younger
- Laugh for no reason
- Read a book recommended by a sister
- Play with your hair
- Do yoga
- Sit on a mat in a quiet space and let go
- Visit a Shaman

By **choosing the checklist,** we can take initiative in our own lives in a gentle way, rather than a forceful one. We can **hold space** for ourselves to prioritize positivity and **Grace.** As you create your own checklist, realize that you are choosing to step into the **Walk of Grace.**

Choosing the Checklist has been pivotal in my journey as I learn how to manage my auto-immune disease. It has allowed the space for me to put my health and well-being as a priority in my life. Rather than bogging my disease down with **Alpha Overdrive** and the **Frenetic Energetic,** as we will get into, I offer myself time and patience as I respect the dis-ease that shares my body.

When we start to choose our checklist we begin to own our **YOU-niqueness** and our **quirks** and **colors.**

So why do we **choose the checklist?** As you take time and find ways to nurture your spirit your **quirks** become your **Colors** and you find **Magic in the Moment.** As we **choose the checklist** we are choosing to step into **Grace.** In this place things begin to unfold without fear or force and we tend to get in our own way. Be sure to cultivate your checklist so that you may appreciate **Progress, not Perfection.** As your checklist develops you will become more comfortable with keeping up with yourself, not the Joneses and **Being the Black Sheep** won't be such a burden anymore. Allow this process to become part of your lifestyle as you embark on your Journey. Take time to choose a checklist that will inspire your spirit and generate **Grace** into your life.

STUCK IN THE MUCK

LIFE IS MEANT TO BE LIVED. So how is it that we often feel like our particular lives are holding us back from doing just that? We are so very busy flitting from one item to the next on the to-do list, that we forget to weigh the value of those tasks. Being busy isn't an accomplishment, and it doesn't make life more meaningful. It's the tasks we choose to busy ourselves with that give it purpose.

So often we end up creating our own chaos when none was necessary, simply because of our ridiculous **expectations.** Like I've said many times before (including just a few pages ago), **Expectation is Resentment in the Making.** Personally, I had a very nebulous expectation that came along with the release of my previous book. I can't even say exactly what it was that I thought was going to happen, but I was pretty sure I was going have to become "something" once it was out in the world. I was so stinking worried. How was I going to live up to being that something? Was I going to be good at it? Was I going to let people down?

Was I going to let myself down? Notice that I had plenty of fears about being an excellent something, despite the fact that I didn't even have a clue as to what that something would be.

I HAD PLENTY OF FEARS ABOUT BEING AN EXCELLENT "SOMETHING"

That, my friends, is how we create our own chaos. And with this added pressure, we push ourselves further into the **Alpha Zone** (which is very, very far away from the Zen Zone we seek), until we are a deer in the headlights. The ridiculous thing is that now we're also the ones driving the truck that's barreling down on us. Ugh. Maybe it's better just not to think of any of it, and put the pedal to the metal!

Recovering Alphaholics are masters at finding distractions: doing the dishes, nagging the kids, raiding the pantry, or stacking project on top of project. Heck, if all else fails, there's always TV, the Internet, and magazines to keep your mind distracted while making you feel even less successful as you create your own chaos by comparing yourself to those shows, web sites, and slick, glossy pages. Not only do you find yourself believing you don't measure up, but you're also likely to start adding even more busy tasks to your to-do list in hopes that someday you will. What a self-defeating cycle. Then you get to follow up all of this feeling bad about yourself by feeding into a concept I call **I'm Bothered that I'm Bothered.**

Not only do these kinds of distractions bring feelings of dis-ease, but they also serve an even more sinister purpose: they steal your time and focus from the purposeful and fulfilling actions you could be taking instead. Rather than meditating, you're online searching for recipes you'll never actually make. Instead of manifesting your dreams, you're standing in the pantry alternating between sweet and salty snacks or over-tidying your space.

SELF-DEFEATING CYCLE: YOU FEEL BAD ABOUT YOURSELF FOR FEELING BAD ABOUT YOURSELF FOR FEELING BAD ABOUT YOURSELF."

The thing is, we feel like we need to keep busy to be worthwhile. We usually have plenty of things that we could/should be doing, but we get overwhelmed by them. So, instead of doing those things, we find other ways to busy ourselves instead. When you pan out from the close-up view we generally take of our own lives, it actually starts to look more than a little silly. Coping mechanisms would be so much handier if they actually helped us to cope well.

It's time to clean the muck out of our lives. F*ck the muck. It causes sabotaging belief systems, self-doubt, and a panic response that carelessly tosses you right back into your old Alpha mindset.

Just as with every recovery process, the **Recovering Alphaholic** may experience the occasional relapse, what I like to call an **Alpha-fall** (rhymes with alcohol), and getting stuck in the muck is often a sign of this. I have found that I get stuck in the noise, in the clutter, in the mire of everyday life, which just leads me further into self doubt. That's where the Alpha kicks in, adding ever more distractions that make the muck thicker and cause me to sink even deeper. The muck is this heavy energetic that keeps us from our becoming. We must step out of it and into **Grace,** but this is easier said than done. The solution I have found and that I share with you is to find a place of quiet. Still the noise, close your eyes to the distractions. Put your energy into following Rumi's advice: The art of knowing is knowing what to ignore.

In our desire to always be busy, it's easy to fall out of the habit of spending quality time with yourself. It becomes so foreign that sometimes we have to write a whole Ah-ha about how to **Choose the Checklist!** Rather than being constantly on the go, bouncing from one event to another before heading off to an appointment and ending the night with a social engagement, consider taking at least a little time to be still. How many moments do you have in your day that are actually **momentful,** meaning you are present, you are aware, and you are engaged only in what is happening right then?

ALWAYS REMEMBER THAT 'BEING' IS EVERY BIT AS MUCH AS A VERB AS 'DOING'

Always remember that 'being' is every bit as much as a verb as 'doing'. The distractions hold no sway over you, and you are clear and focused about what you are doing. Not only that, but as a **Recovering Alpha Female,** I can attest that it's actually OK not to leave the house sometimes. In fact, it's even OK to enjoy it! Forget about FOMO (fear of missing out), and embrace **JOMO** (Joy Of Missing Out) instead.

Remember that you can not only turn to graceful feminine leaders around you, but you can also be one for others. We can support one another, reminding each other to f*ck the muck and allow the path to unfold. By holding space for one another, we are able to respect the situation of another while also helping guide them, and ourselves. Kindness is contagious, so remember that when you are kinder to yourself, you are kinder to others. That is my intention for you with this book. Additionally, don't forget to hold space for yourself, as this is what allows you to accept the muck of the situation and give yourself the **Grace** to step out of it.

So, what is your muck? What is busying your mind and your body and keeping you from living as your kinder self? When we are driven by fear (of failure, embarrassment, judgment, criticism, etc.), we end up filling our lives with muck. However, when there is a goal, a dream, or a passion that you know is worthwhile, then it's imperative to get out of the muck. It's time to put your faith forward to be your best self and let go of attachment to the outcome.

MANAGE YOUR OWN STUFF

EVERY DAY WE DEAL WITH STUFF. There's **stuff** to do, **stuff** to take care of, and **stuff** to think about. Sometimes, though, we forget the importance of managing our own **stuff** and get caught up in trying to fix or solve someone else's **stuff.** If each of us could focus on our own issues rather than others', I am confident we would see positive change on a global level. Each of us needs to find the wherewithal to manage our own energies, to keep them aligned so that our thoughts and actions may be clear.

Of course, our human condition—especially for us Alpha Females—leads us to want to solve others' dilemmas, even to drive others' thinking. When it comes to any kind of drama, it's so tempting to limit and try to influence the outcome. We want to be in charge, to fix things in our family, at work, and in social situations. Our colors are vibrant and we tend to push them onto others instead of letting them unfold on their own.

Think of the Alpha Mom who pushes her kids to join the right clubs, take the right classes, or excel in sports, even when it might not be the best choice for the child. Or the Alpha Wife who wants her spouse to dress just right to project that perfect-on-paper image she thinks is appropriate. Sometimes the Alpha Female even finds herself pushing friends or neighbors to follow her religious beliefs, all the while convincing herself that she's just trying to help them. Operating from this place of control and judgment, however, is simply not authentic. **The Recovering Alphaholic** strives to accept others for who they are and to meet them where they are in their own journeys. She remains **YOU-nique** by encouraging rather than by imposing force and judgment.

Let's be real, here. You can only get away with directing other people's **stuff** for so long, anyway, before it starts to hurt your relationships. I once had someone close share with me about a friendship she'd developed with a man. **Recovering Alphaholic** me got all judgy-judgy and decided the relationship was an inappropriate one for a married woman. Of course, my judgments put me right into the Create Your Own Chaos camp, which is pretty much never a good idea. Interestingly, when you get all up in someone else's business, you get stuck in their muck. Again, not a good idea, and in my case, it damaged an important relationship in my life for a long time. On a related note, managing my own **stuff** has been integral to managing my disease.

When you manage your own **stuff,** you are able to act with integrity, **Grace,** and acceptance. That is when you find yourself

WHEN YOU GET UP IN SOMEONE ELSE'S BUSINESS, YOU GET STUCK IN THEIR MUCK

extending that **Grace** to others and therefore honoring it in yourself as well. You allow others to display their own colors so they can be fully themselves. By owning and managing your own energy you inspire others to authentically manage their **stuff.**

When you own up to a mistake, it lowers the pressure on someone else to puff themselves up to try and meet whatever **expectations** they think you have.

Alpha Females are often so quick to point fingers, delegate, volun-tell their spouse, accuse, judge, label, etc. Most often, these actions are done in the name of efficiency and productivity, but it's still managing someone else's stuff and will drive you to distraction. This is where the **Peace Ring** comes in. As we notice ourselves pointing that judgmental finger outward we become increasingly aware that there are three fingers on our own hand pointing back at ourselves.

Wearing the **Peace Ring** on the index finger changes the negative cycle. With patience and practice it transforms into a circuit of positivity. Instead of pointing out someone's flaws we point out their beautiful, **YOU-nique** qualities, which, in turn, points three fingers back at our own amazing quirks and colors.

By placing Peace on that accusatory finger we manifest peace in our lives. We transform a negative communication circuit into a loving environment where we may **hold space** for one another. **Peacing It All Together** is about transformation. It is about outward kindness, reflection instead of reaction, and leading from the heart not the head.

This has been an ongoing lesson for me. As a **Recovering Alpha** it has been a choice to resist the compulsion to fix what I intuit as being somehow wrong, such as another's opinion or lifestyle.

One means of learning to better manage your own **stuff** is through an understanding of the chakras. Yes, it does take us back into that Woo-Woo realm, but considering the fact that each of these energies lies within you, they provide a useful framework for exploring how to manage a variety of interactions, both internal and external. It's likely no coincidence that color plays such an important part of the way I tend to see things and to communicate, as chakras are often depicted through the use of color. As with so many things, explanations about chakras can go from super-simple to extremely complex, depending on how far down the rabbit hole you'd like to dive. We're going to stick with a fairly simple description of aspects that have helped me on my healing journey. But if you find that it strikes a chord with you, feel free to follow up with other resources and maybe find your own **Woo-Woo Guru** to help guide the way.

Chakras are swirling wheels of energy (or data banks for the left brainers) within our bodies that correspond to our lives in different ways. As you work up from the base of the spine to the top of the head, there are seven different chakras.

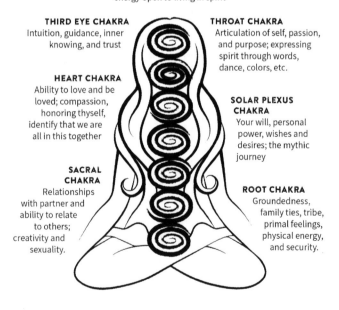

CROWN CHAKRA
Connection to nature, the divine, the unexplainable; creation energy open to living in spirit

THIRD EYE CHAKRA
Intuition, guidance, inner knowing, and trust

THROAT CHAKRA
Articulation of self, passion, and purpose; expressing spirit through words, dance, colors, etc.

HEART CHAKRA
Ability to love and be loved; compassion, honoring thyself, identify that we are all in this together

SOLAR PLEXUS CHAKRA
Your will, personal power, wishes and desires; the mythic journey

SACRAL CHAKRA
Relationships with partner and ability to relate to others; creativity and sexuality.

ROOT CHAKRA
Groundedness, family ties, tribe, primal feelings, physical energy, and security.

THE SEVEN CHAKRAS

Each chakra has many other characteristics subscribed to it, such as a gemstone, an element, a color, or even a sound. This topic goes incredibly deep, being followed and discussed for thousands of years, so if it resonates with you, find a **Woo-Woo Guru** to assist in discovery and expansion.

The focus of this brief introduction to chakras is to remind us to look around and see whatever signs our lives

OUR BODIES SIGNAL TO US WHAT IS OUT OF BALANCE, IT'S OUR JOB TO RECOGNIZE THEM

are showing us to signal that things are out of balance. Once we learn to recognize these signs, each of us can then seek new ways to **Manage Your Own Stuff.** Taking responsibility in this way can be a gift toward living a more **Zentered** life.

Chakras are informative energy centers in the body (I like to use the analogy of databanks) that I exercise as a resource to check in with myself when I find my Alpha spinning out in the Frenetic Energetic. This method of organization is an energetic way to assess what issues or personal beliefs are up for you or what limitations you have outgrown and how your body can help inform you!

The word chakra means "wheel" in Sanskrit because the energy operates much like a wheel in your daily life, turning, opening, or closing, depending on the situation. Because each chakra—or center of energy—corresponds to a particular place in your body, it is not uncommon to find challenges or issues with any one chakra which might manifest into disease or physical difficulties in your body.

The concept of chakras certainly stretched my Alpha nature in the beginning. But, staying open and embracing the possibilities of alternative healing has been pivotal in managing my auto-immune disease, MS. This disease has the potential to be crippling, but instead it gave me the strength to manage my own **stuff,** own up to my authentic self, and listen to my body's innate wisdom.

QUIRKS MAKE
YOU COLORFUL

EVEN THE WORD ITSELF IS CUTE: QUIRK. It's snappy and whimsical and packs a lot of meaning into one short syllable. **Quirks** are those things that you do just a little differently than most everybody else; they are peculiar behavioral habits. **Quirks** make you **YOU-nique!** Perhaps you have a loud and unusual laugh, maybe you have a habit of not using contractions when you speak, or it could be that you can't fall asleep if your arm or leg extends over the edge of the bed. Sometimes people feel like these things make them weird or unlikeable and often perceive their **quirks** as something negative.

YOUR QUIRKS MAKE YOU YOU-NIQUE!

I used to be so embarrassed by some of my **quirks** that I literally avoided doing things I enjoyed rather than run the risk of someone thinking I was weird. I very much like to unwind and relax in a hot tub, whether as a lone activity where I focus on how good the water feels on my tired muscles, or as a group activity where everyone spends time chatting (and usually comparing previous hot tub experiences, for some reason). Unfortunately, one of my **quirks** shines its lovely little light whenever I get in a hot tub: jazz hands! For some reason, my brain does not want my hands to be wet when I'm in a hot tub (maybe it's worried I'll need to scratch my nose or answer an important call from the President), and I therefore sit in the water, both arms bent at the elbow,

I WOULD AVOID DOING THINGS I ENJOYED BECAUSE I WAS EMBARRASSED BY MY QUIRKS

hands sticking out above the surface with my fingers spread like a cheerleader who has something to prove.

My personal **quirks** have even impacted how friends and I interact with one another. One of my life-long friends makes a point to always park her vehicle somewhere other than my driveway, simply because she knows that I get really bummed when there are oil spots on the concrete. This friend has her own awesome **quirks,** though, that make her just as weird and wonderful as mine make me. Together and separately, we have learned what it means to own your **quirks.**

While we're busy worrying about how these **quirks** and traits make us different from other people, we often forget that being different from other people is actually a pretty great thing. When you start to identify and examine your **quirks,** things can get really interesting. When it's a behavioral **quirk,** for example, it can be fascinating to explore and determine how you came to have it. There's a good chance that the story behind your **quirk** is a pretty good subplot in the story of your life.

- If you hold your breath every time you go through a tunnel or lift your feet when driving over railroad tracks, you can probably trace those behaviors back to fun times spent in the car as a child with siblings, friends, or cousins.

- Someone who always puts coffee mugs away with the handles facing the same direction might realize that they do so not just because of how it looks, but because it's more efficient. More mugs fit in the cupboard, and you always know where to grab for the handle.

- When someone asks you the time, do you tell them precisely what your watch says, or do you round to the nearest minute? The nearest five minutes? Why did you decide somewhere along the way that this is how you prefer to do it?

With all of that said, remember that knowing the "why" of your **quirks** is not nearly as important as accepting them. Searching for a reason you do something can lead down a path that you'd rather avoid, either because it takes you to an unhealthy place (reliving trauma, for example)

KNOWING THE "WHY" OF YOUR QUIRKS IS NOT AS IMPORTANT AS ACCEPTING THEM

or because it simply removes you from the current moment. If tracking down the origin of your **quirks** is fun, that's great. If it's a burden, or it distracts you from the important business of living your life, then it requires you to put too much energy in the wrong place. Asking "why" only complicates things and prevents acceptance.

It's common for us (or others) to label our **quirks** as flaws or negative. Stepping into **Grace** gives us the opportunity to reevaluate how we view them. The idea is that once you recognize your **quirks** for what they are, it becomes far easier to own them and to move from judgment to acceptance. Picking at your fingernail cuticles when you're nervous can go from being an embarrassing tic to being something that makes you more colorful. It becomes one of your **YOU-nique** qualities.

ONCE YOU RECOGNIZE YOUR QUIRKS FOR WHAT THEY ARE, IT'S EASIER TO OWN THEM AND MOVE FORWARD

Keep in mind that a whole lot of our **quirks** are actually coping mechanisms that we have developed over time. Maybe you always do your hair before your makeup because that's the way it worked best when you were a kid sharing a bathroom with your sister. Or maybe you always read a magazine from start to finish rather than skipping around because you found that was the best way to keep your place during constant interruptions during college.

And what if you examine your **quirks** and find something you just truly do not like? (Like, say, that **quirky** habit I picked up of biting my nails when processing or when I am anxious.) In those circumstances, you have some options. You can try to remove or refine the **quirk** or you can **hold space** and allow for it, moving forward with acceptance. This is living with **Grace.**

Far too often, we fall into the trap of self-deprecation where we think of our **quirks** as flaws or of believing others who see them that way. You end up feeling insecure, and whether someone else is pointing them out, or you're just feeling particularly self-conscious, these things that are really beautiful and **YOU-nique** parts of your character or appearance don't get the credit they deserve.

As a **Recovering Alphaholic** it's time to recognize that your **quirks** make you colorful. They are the flashes of violet and indigo hinting to the world that you are a queen; the purple of your passion. They are the warm orange and gold of your comfort with intimacy. They're the spring green of your perennial humor and, yes, even the glowing-hot red of your temper. Sure, things are almost always easier when they're black and white, but they're not nearly as beautiful. Embrace your **quirks** - they make you colorful. Once you own your **quirks** you have the colorful creative freedom to express your **YOUique** self.

BE THE BLACK SHEEP

THE IMAGE OF SHEEP COMES UP A LOT IN OUR VERNACULAR. When someone is blindly following another instead of thinking for themselves, we say they are being sheep. When someone is hiding their real intentions by pretending to be part of the group, they are a wolf in sheep's clothing. It seems like we don't really have all that high of an opinion of sheep. I mean, they're so boring that we count them to fall asleep.

THERE'S ONE SHEEP THAT'S NEVER BORING: THE BLACK SHEEP

There's one sheep that's never boring, though: **The Black Sheep. The Black Sheep** of the family is the one who never quite fits in. Usually, there's a negative connotation involved, as if they don't fit in because of something ranging from naughty to downright evil. **The Black Sheep** is the great uncle that ran off to the hippie commune or the sister who skipped college and went right into a blue-collar job when the rest of the siblings followed in their parents' footsteps as doctors.

As people, we're pretty hardwired to want to fit in. We need community to survive and to thrive. In addition to that, our desire to fit in with our own families is a biological drive that has kept our species on the planet this long. In our current age, we can generally survive without family, but that doesn't simply switch off our innate desire to belong.

IT TAKES A LOT OF GRACE TO REALIZE THAT YOU DISAGREE WITHOUT PLACING BLAME OR FEELING RESENTFUL THAT THINGS COULD BE DIFFERENT.

The path to becoming a **RAF** often requires us to make different choices than those our families expect us to make. After all, they're part of what formed that original Alpha Female persona to begin with. You were learning the lessons taught to you. Some were intentional and some were not. When you choose to live your life differently, family can interpret it as rejection.

To be honest, sometimes being **the Black Sheep** does stem from rejection of the culture in which you've been steeped, whether you're talking about your family, your workplace, your church, or the greater community in which you live. For me, one of the hardest parts was that I did find myself judging my family and disagreeing with certain aspects of their beliefs and values. It takes a lot of **Grace** to realize that you disagree without placing blame or feeling resentful that things could be different.

I have been incredibly blessed to come from a wonderful family. I have three siblings, all of whom are accomplished individuals with amazing, generous souls, led by an Alpha father and an Omega mother. Despite not having a handbook on how to raise successful children, they did an incredible job. So, when I began to separate myself from aspects of my upbringing, there was some guilt and a sense that maybe I no longer belonged.

Interestingly, when I explained to my brother that I felt as if I were **the Black Sheep** of the family, he shared that he felt the same way about himself. Later, my sister revealed that she, too, felt as if she were **the Black Sheep** of the family. Each of us had our own **quirks** (colors) that we thought made us too different, that somehow kept us separate from the group.

These conversations helped me to realize that those things that made us **YOU-nique** individuals were not shortcomings at all. In painting, black can be created by combining all of the colors of the rainbow. It's not a coincidence that combining the colors of your **quirks** can lead to being a **Black Sheep.** Accepting this in ourselves helps us get to a place where we can support one another and even celebrate being those **Black Sheep.** When we accept that in ourselves, it's so much easier to accept it in others and to step into that **Place of Grace.**

IT'S NOT A COINCIDENCE THAT COMBINING THE COLORS OF YOUR QUIRKS CAN LEAD TO BEING A BLACK SHEEP

Allowing yourself to be **the Black Sheep** isn't just about family relationships, though. Instead, it's about choosing to live with acceptance. It's about letting your heart lead you **faith-forward** where it needs to go. The Alpha Female has a well-curated public persona, showing the world what she thinks it wants to see. Stripping that away and presenting yourself as you truly are leaves you incredibly vulnerable, which is not at all comfortable. Often, your true self turns out to be a **Black Sheep.**

In the old Alpha mindset, being **the Black Sheep** meant being recognized for the wrong reasons. It was negative, possibly even shameful. Once we allow ourselves to let that go, being **the Black Sheep** becomes something wonderful. It means celebrating all of the colors that make you **YOU-nique** and honoring them in your words and actions every day. Additionally, remember to **hold space** for other **Black Sheep** to celebrate their **YOU-nique** colors.

We typically want to be someone that makes our parents proud. We want ridiculously for our families to approve of our choices and the lives we lead. Sometimes, though, that doesn't allow us to honor our true sense of self or to follow the call of spirit. Instead of shying away from authenticity, however, the **RAF** makes the call to live with trust, purpose, and passion. If that means becoming **the Black Sheep,** well then, so be it.

MAGIC IN THE MOMENT

THE BEAUTY OF THIS AH-HA IS THAT IT GIVES US PERMISSION TO LET LIFE UNFOLD AS WE LIVE IN THE MAGIC OF EACH MOMENT. It's about not scheduling every minute of the day or judging your worth by the number of check marks on a to-do list.

Relishing the **Magic in the Moment** allows you to be still, to witness the world and the miracles it unveils from instant to instant. It grounds us to our reality and reminds us that we are part of something so much bigger than ourselves.

BE STILL, WITNESS THE WORLD AND IT'S MIRACLES, WE ARE PART OF SOMETHING SO MUCH BIGGER THAN OURSELVES

There are countless things around us at all times that we barely understand, and taking an opportunity to go just a little deeper with our thinking can expand our patience and perception incredibly. I like to use the example of one of the giants of the online world known as Amazon.com. We open up the web site and think we have it all figured out. You can search for stuff you want, order it, and pay. Easy peasy. This is pretty much all we really need to know to be able to use Amazon.com to get what we need or want.

TAKING AN OPPORTUNITY TO GO DEEPER WITH OUR THINKING CAN EXPAND OUR PATIENCE AND PERCEPTION

But, if you take a step back and further contemplate Amazon.com, there is so much more that could be understood. First of all, how does all that computer code work, and who programmed it? What about the people involved in the process of shipping your product to you? Is it all just automated by machines? Heck, what about the product itself? Where was it made and by whom and with what materials? The sheer number of people between the raw materials and the product being delivered to your door is a wonder in and of itself. Where does the cardboard for the box come from? Every object, every creature, and every idea has the potential to absolutely blow our minds with the details that usually go unnoticed.

When we are fully in the moment, we come from a place where we accept that there is so much we do not know or understand, and it can cause an immense sense of wonder. To be present to whatever you're doing, rather than worrying about what you need to do next, means it's suddenly possible to just bathe in the small nuances. We get to spend a small time in a quiet place where everything is magic and miracles. This is what it means to be in **flow.**

"The only true wisdom is knowing that we know nothing." - Socrates

Most of us can't justify living in this state all the time, but the rarity with which we visit it is a cause for concern. We could spend every second attempting to be productive or to earn the admiration of others, but there's so much really great stuff that gets overlooked when we have this sort of tunnel vision. So, my approach was to start small.

When I first began my journey as a **Recovering Alpha Female,** most of my energy was expended on meeting external commitments and **expectations** and learning to manage my MS diagnosis. At first I was only able to carve out a few minutes in a day where I could let my mind loose to actually explore the moment I was in and be curious. I would have a little time to notice my surroundings and to wonder. What if? Why does? When did? Instead of marching from one thing to the next, checking the check list, I occasionally gave myself permission to stroll around a bit, to interact with the moment just as it was. I was learning to see the **Magic in the Moment.**

THE VERY QUESTIONS WE SEEK TO AVOID ARE THE ONES THAT CAN BRING US THE MOST INSIGHT

As I became more practiced, I would sometimes find an afternoon where I didn't have every moment racked and stacked, and during those times I made a choice to discover the **Magic in the Moment.** Sometime after that, I was actually creating these situations, even putting aside a whole weekend where I did not have a plan, a schedule, or a list of problems to solve or fix. This is something that is easier said than done, of course. We **Recovering Alphaholics** have often, consciously or subconsciously, designed our overly busy lives for the purpose of avoiding these kinds of quiet times. It can feel a lot safer to be "busy" and distracted than to let your mind start questioning things.

The paradox of it is that the very questions we seek to avoid are the ones that can bring us the most insight and lead to authenticity. You can run but you cannot hide from your thoughts. To be fair, personal satisfaction for most probably doesn't come directly from contemplating who mined the ore or how many people it took to build and ship the Kindle you just ordered, it is in this time of focus that we become aware of the magic. But there are other questions and realizations that are finally able to come to the surface when you've gotten into the habit of accepting any given moment for what is. It is in this space of quiet that we get to know our knowing.

IT CAN FEEL SAFER TO BE BUSY AND DISTRACTED

The beauty of one moment can have its own meaning, but it also opens us up for future revelations. In my case, I was really starting to understand the need to find **Magic in the Moment** after my divorce and diagnosis. I had found a new sweetheart who unfortunately lived on the other side of the state. When I wanted to see him, I had to get time off work, arrange care for my children, and purchase a ticket. In many ways, it added even more stress to my already overly busy and financially strapped life. However, taking that time started to feel like a gift I was giving to myself.

THE LOVE LOOP

GIVING TO OTHERS IS SOMETHING I'VE ALWAYS UNDERSTOOD ON A PRETTY FUNDAMENTAL LEVEL. I adore the words of St. Francis when he said, "It is in giving that you receive." I have always found incredible joy in giving to others. In the case of traveling to see my sweetheart, I recognized that it made me happy to give this time to myself. Somewhere along the line, though, the moments of quiet that I was learning to gift myself would give rise to some of those not so comfortable questions.

SOMETIMES IT IS EQUALLY IMPORTANT TO RECEIVE AS IT IS TO GIVE

I had always taken to the idea that it was good and right to give, give, give. "'Tis better to give than receive" and the aforementioned quote from St. Francis summed up my beliefs fairly well, and I think most of us were raised with similar ideas. Heck, when we're on an airplane, we literally have to be told to take care of ourselves first in the case of an emergency. After all, if you don't put your own oxygen mask on, you're not going to stay conscious long enough to help other people get theirs on! Still, questioning beliefs about giving and receiving can feel selfish, since we all know it's greedy and uncouth to wish to receive gifts, whether they be material goods or simply someone's attention. With my greater ability to ask questions, though, I was able to start to understand some advice given to me by a beautiful soul sister, Sohini, who introduced me to the idea that sometimes it is equally as important to receive as to give. Say what?!

Those are the kinds of thoughts I would normally have crowded out of my mind with shopping lists and kids' sport schedules and strategizing my latest work project. But, in being willing to be in the moment, I had opened myself up to entertaining the thoughts that I hadn't previously allowed in. What could she have meant in saying it might be equally as important to recieve as to give? By listening to her words and providing myself with time to examine and understand them, I came to see how important it is to allow someone to give to you. So often we deflect receiving as an act of humility.

First of all, you're worth it. There is no reason to be overly coy about it other than to meet our particular culture's made up rules about how to behave when given a gift. "Oh, you shouldn't have…" "No, I couldn't possibly…" "It's too much…" When you say those things, what are you telling that person about your worth? More importantly, what are you telling yourself about your worth? I'm clearly not advocating that you become a narcissist, but when our default is to diminish our own value, it might be a **cause for pause.**

Secondly, think of how good it feels when you give someone a gift that they truly appreciate. It's a wonderful feeling that can be almost euphoric. How cool is it to give that feeling to someone else by graciously accepting their gift to you? This creates a **Love Loop** in which we support one another; we see each other's value alongside our own. I give to you because I care about you, and it strengthens our relationship. Out of that closer bond you feel the desire to give to me. The gift cycle is endless, and I wear an infinity symbol around my neck daily to remind me to both give and receive genuinely.

It is in giving that we receive AND it is receiving that we give!

the LOVE LOOP

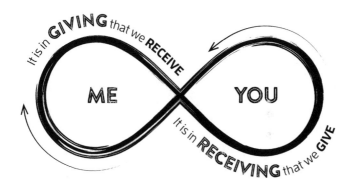

"We make a living by what we get, but we make a life by what we give." This quote (often attributed to Winston Churchill) makes a lot of sense when you consider the importance of both giving and receiving. Choose to give lovingly, and you will receive gifts lovingly given to you. You keep this loop alive and active by graciously receiving. Spread positive energy, and positivity will come back to you. How wonderful that in making yourself happy, you can brighten the world for others, and vice versa - you get what you give, so give good!

GET ON THE BETTER-THAN PLAN

IN OUR FAST-PACE, AMPED-UP, RAMPED-UP, INSTANT GRATIFICATION SOCIETY, EXPECTATIONS OF IMMEDIACY CAN BE A MAJOR HUMBLING BLOCK. We want what we want, and we want it now. Moreover, as Alphaholics, we're also pretty good at figuring out how to get what we want, which often translates into taking care of it ourselves. When I'm in **Alpha Overdrive,** I work my butt off, and I expect immediate results and success. When do I need to be the best? ALL THE TIME!

As a **Recovering Alpha Female,** however, I've learned to look at things differently. In fact, I've learned that I have to look at things differently if I'm going to honor myself and manage the disease that shares my body. One place that I've found incredible inspiration to better regulate myself and operate from a **Place of Grace** is through the words of one of my greatest **Woo-Woo Gurus,** the late Wayne Dyer, who said, "True nobility is not about being better than anyone else, it's about being better than you used to be."

Wow, does that take a lot of the pressure off! I tend to dream big, and then to pour my heart and soul into what I do. Creating my non-profit, *Underground Kindness*, for example, has filled me with love, drained me of tears, and bolstered my self confidence before destroying my self confidence before bolstering it once again. Publishing my books has caused me to bully myself until I was certain I couldn't do it, and left

YOU DON'T NEED TO BE BETTER THAN ANYONE ELSE. YOU JUST NEED TO BE BTTER THAN YOU USED TO BE

me beaming with pride when I held the beautiful first print in my hand, and then taken me through pretty much every conceivable emotion and back.

In championing this movement toward recovery from the Alpha lifestyle, there have been times that I have just wanted to throw in the towel. To reach the right people at the right time with the right message? It's daunting. Most infuriatingly, it's a really long, slow process. Patience is not my natural state of being. As I learn to walk in **Grace,** patience is a new muscle that I am starting to exercise. **Patience takes practice.** I have never liked to do things slowly. When I make a long-term plan for something, I'm usually thinking in months, not years! So, when I can't just put my vision out to the world and move on to the next stage, I feel diminished.

That is, until I realize that I am literally living every aspect of what I'm sharing. When I started this book, I was very much **Stuck in the Muck.** I was struggling with whether to keep going or to just stop, and the thing that was holding me up was the fact that I'm not done yet. Let me lay out my line of thinking here, and maybe you can relate:

"Holy S***. Why does it take so long to share this thing that took me years to learn and that is based on moving forward slowly and intentionally?! Are we there yet?"

The fact of the matter is that trying to be the best, or the first, or the fastest is exhausting, and there's really only one person who gets the title in the end. Everyone else can be setting themselves up for disappointment. In Ah-has for *The Recovering Alpha Female,* I talked about the importance of **Progress, Not Perfection,** and the **Better-Than Plan** is an excellent way to implement this belief in your life.

The concept is simple, you don't have to be the best, as long as you're willing to be a little better than you were the day before. If I'm being totally honest here (I am), there are times I have to strive to be a little better from moment to moment, because life can get overwhelming. I have come to embrace what's next, own it and hold space for **Progress, Not Perfection.** This is progress and I've done a little better. Maybe yesterday you yelled at your kids three times, and today you only yelled once. Is it the best? Not really. Is it better than yesterday? Heck, yeah! And tomorrow you'll do even better.

This concept of doing a little at a time will likely seem boring and unsatisfying, especially since you're probably used to going full throttle. Accepting, embracing, and acknowledging that discomfort is a part of the process and is a step in moving toward **Grace.** You're teaching your brain a whole new way of doing things, and it starts with incubating this new mindset. You're not used to congratulating yourself for doing such an average amount of work toward a final goal, and it sometimes feels as if you are patronizing yourself.

When I was 38 I thought I should make a hike in 38 minutes to the top. Now, I'm happy if I get out and hike halfway or go all the way but at a slower pace.

Take time to know your **Better-Than Plan** and know your benchmarks.

Part of dealing with this discomfort, in addition to simply holding space for it, is to remember what you are gaining. You're refusing to remain **Stuck in the Muck.** You are giving yourself the chance to **Manage Your Stuff.** You're creating spaces in your day where it is possible to look for the **Magic in the Moment.** It takes a major shift in thinking because we are so used to running as hard and as fast as we can to "accomplish" something. With the **Better-Than Plan,** self-satisfaction becomes natural. It **flows** freely, and we come to discover that we are aiming for a **Place of Grace** in the mind and body. It's OK for things to take time. Remember, we're looking for **Progress, not Perfection.**

ALPHA OVERDRIVE
A Way of Armoring the Alpha

THE ALPHA FEMALE KICKS ASS. She's charismatic and charming and knows how to put together a step-by-step plan to make things happen. These are amazing qualities, and someone blessed with these abilities should get to enjoy the sense of satisfaction that comes with doing a job and doing it well. Like all things, however, these qualities require balance. Going too far in any direction usually ends up being bad, bad news for our **Recovering Alphaholic.**

Last spring I found myself desperately **Stuck in the Muck.** One book was already published, speaking engagements were continuing, and it was clearly time to make a move forward with my business. So, did I put together a nice plan to reach my goals and then follow each action step in order to hit milestones and objectives at a reasonable pace?

No, no I did not.

Instead I dilly-dallied with website design. I agonized over branding elements and matters that were really pretty trivial in the grand scheme of things. I focused my energy on my to-do lists, my children's schedules, finding the best deal on a certain item, and possibly going back and forth to the pantry more times than was reasonable. I was busy for the sake of being busy. Clearly, I needed to get unstuck. It suddenly became imperative to do all of the things and to do them all now and to do them all perfectly and quickly and affordably...and, and, and!

In true Alpha form, I overcompensated. I was running from sun-up to sun-down trying to be a mover and a shaker. I have a proven track record of getting things done that way, after all.

IN TRUE ALPHA FORM, I OVERCOMPENSATED

As I mentioned before, patiently waiting for things to unfold in their own time is really not my strong suit. I had gone from zero to a hundred miles an hour, throwing the engine into **Alpha Overdrive.** Surely that was the way to get myself back on track, right?

What we often forget in **Alpha Overdrive** is that this is the climate where disease loves to grow.

Alpha Overdrive might have worked in my previous life but simply making myself busy isn't enough to fool me or my body for long these days. I found myself with plenty to do, but not a whole lot was actually getting accomplished when it came to working towards my best self. This is a pattern that

I FOUND MYSELF WITH PLENTY TO DO, BUT NOT A WHOLE LOT WAS ACTUALLY GETTING ACCOMPLISHED

we often resort to, and as a **Recovering Alphaholic,** I'm grateful to say that I am more aware of myself, my thoughts, and my actions (which is the key to change according to Ghandi). Focusing on the details but not really making progress was a means to keep myself from feeling, thinking, and above all trusting. When I didn't like the way it felt to be **Stuck in the Muck,** I skipped right past the part where I figured out why I was in that place, instead armoring myself as I always had.

When you armor up, you put your body in a place of constriction. In this place, you don't get adequate blood flow, nutrient supplies, or movement; which can lead to a number of health issues such as high blood pressure, autoimmune disease, and more. MS is a sleeping giant in my body, and it's so easy to overlook when I've shifted into **Alpha Overdrive.** Of course, the result is an undesired flare up of symptoms.

When an Alpha is trying to move something forward and it's not cruising right along, she tends to distract herself with the checklist. "I know..." her brain says. "Instead of allowing this process to happen naturally, I'm going to get myself completely bogged down in perfectionism. That'll give me plenty of excuses not to figure out why things aren't moving forward." It's all about putting on the armor and reverting to old coping patterns while attempting to find validation.

SHE JUST DOESN'T HAVE THAT BEAUTIFUL, COMPASSIONATE SOFTER SIDE THAT ACTS AS HOME BASE FOR YOUR AUTHENTIC, GRACEFUL SELF

Something to keep in mind regarding this **Alpha Overdrive** is that even if it does get some results, it has to be balanced. It can be a helpful tool because sometimes you have to let the boss-lady out to kick some ass, but it's not a long-term strategy anymore. She just doesn't have that beautiful, compassionate softer side that acts as home base for her authentic, graceful self. As someone who has plenty of experience vacillating between both approaches, I can tell you without a doubt that true purpose and positive action is almost exclusively the domain of the gentle, authentic self, rather than that of **Alpha Overdrive.**

When you do find yourself in overdrive, it's time to do some evaluation. First of all, you need to determine if it's helping or hindering. Don't just look at your life or your project and confuse being busy with being productive. Instead, go back to your heart whispers. What are your intentions? Are you coming from a place of **Grace?** Does it feel good or are they merely forced? Once you have determined that **Alpha Overdrive** is not (or is no longer) benefitting you, slam that sucker into neutral and center yourself. It's a good idea to take this step back for evaluation because even though it's sometimes necessary to armor the Alpha, this act can trigger a chain reaction that leads us right into **Alpha Overdrive.** The next thing you know, you're back to worrying about what **They** will think and you miss out on true authentic connections in a mad dash to be everything to everyone.

This is the time to take a break and replenish your internal fortitude. You could even start with something as simple as lying in the grass connecting to the wisdom of days gone by or getting a massage to **Zenter** yourself. To **Zenter** is to bring yourself back into balance, to plug into your authentic self and recharge. Either you've just accomplished something awesome, or you've stopped yourself from letting **Alpha Overdrive** take you off course. Either way, good for you! Now is the time to do something that refuels you. Meditation might be a good way to clear your mind, while a walk or run can help work out some pent-up energy.

Whatever works best for you, take this chance to **Zenter** and get out of **Alpha Overdrive.** Give yourself the well-earned opportunity to revitalize. The extra minutes you give to yourself are a gift of **Grace** that will help you to rebalance and approach your thoughts with intention.

FRENETIC ENERGETIC

AS AN ALPHA FEMALE, YOU NATURALLY FEEL THINGS DEEPLY. Your emotions are extreme, and sometimes you try to ignore or minimize them by focusing on a seemingly endless parade of distractions. In fact, you're kind of addicted to it. As a **Recovering Alpha Female,** however, you have begun to align your energies and learn that living with **Grace** is a lifestyle choice: to have an understanding of what you want to contribute to the world, as well as a set of skills that have always helped you to get things done. This can be a very useful combination, but it can also send you back into **Alpha Overdrive.**

As you become more balanced, you begin to see how we are all interconnected. You recognize the importance behind the causes you believe in and find yourself driven to make things better or to help others see what your eyes have been opened to. The next thing you know, you're trying to pull your friends, family, and neighbors into your **stuff.** Your history of scheduling, planning, kicking ass and taking names presents itself as a handy way to campaign for your cause.

Falling prey to this pattern is what I refer to as **Frenetic Energetic.** Something that is frenetic is moving quickly, often in a wild and uncontrolled way. Why, that sounds a whole lot like what's going on in Alpha Overdrive, doesn't it? Oftentimes when we step into the Frenetic Energetic, we end up turning our cause into a crisis. To be fair, our causes really can be crises. Perhaps you have been drawn to a social justice issue that has very real, negative implications for people. Our Alpha tendencies push us to try to solve, fix, or mend the problem. It's all about taking action.

SOMETIMES THE BEST WAY TO PROMOTE YOUR CAUSE IS THROUGH INSPIRATION, NOT INFORMATION

The **Recovering Alphaholic** has to remember that sometimes the best way to promote your cause is through inspiration, not information. It's perfectly reasonable to want to share all the Why? and How come? of your causes, but that's not always the best way to help them. When we get too attached to sharing the information, we can actually end up in the way of bringing about the solution. Information can be a turn-off. Inspiration, though, is the exact opposite. Instead of preaching, you're leading by love and example;

and this is what allows the necessary space and **Grace** for others to unfold.

LEADING BY LOVE AND EXAMPLE GIVES OTHERS THE SPACE TO UNFOLD

For example, you may have recognized a desire to rebuild family connections and to heal old relationship wounds. This is likely a noble objective and one that you may feel you can champion. Unfortunately, not everyone is going to respond the way you would like to your attempts at "fixing" things. Rather than forcing others into awkward situations they will resent, it might be necessary to give that relationship space, to accept it for what it is, and to be less firmly attached to a particular outcome. You might also choose to go about taking steps toward mending your own relationships without worrying about whether or not others are doing the same. When you remove yourself from the shackles of what **They** think, it gives the people around you permission to do the same. Inspiration, not information. (Notice, too, how this requires you to **Manage Your Own Stuff.)**

On the other hand, getting bogged down in the details of the backstory can all too easily turn our cause into a crisis. Focusing too much on "why" is one of the sneakiest ways we have of creating our own chaos. Approaching a cause with the **Frenetic Energetic** can fill it with unattainable **expectations,** turn others away from your purpose, and lead to burnout for you. As it is with all things, there must be balance. The balance to **Frenetic Energetic** is living with **Grace.**

THE BALANCE TO FRENETIC ENERGETIC IS LIVING WITH GRACE

That **Grace** extends both to others and to yourself and allows you to move forward from the authentic heart instead of from a place of urgency. The **Frenetic Energetic** funnels us right into **Alpha Overdrive.** Instead of walking a path with compassion and kindness, we sprint blindly, tripping and grasping on to the fear of missing out.

We see the **Frenetic Energetic** all around us in society. Look no further than the salesman who is pushing way too hard for his cause, to the point that you are pushed away by that energy. There's a difference between someone who is outgoing and enthusiastic about a cause and someone who is consumed by it. The **Frenetic Energetic** is always there. It's up to us to choose not to jump into it and to be aware.

I WORRY THAT I WORRY TOO MUCH

IN THE PAST, I HAVE ENCOURAGED ALL OF US RAFS TO LOOK UP TO OUR YOUNGERS. This particular ah-ha is a result of paying attention to my oldest son and learning from him. He is intelligent and responsible, and as the oldest child, he sometimes takes on the roles of caretaker, peacemaker, or grounding force. The manner in which he does these things is often thought provoking to me. Sometimes the traits that he reveals about himself reveal a lot about most of us.

Not too long ago, during a conversation with my son, I noted that he seemed to have a lot on his mind. Wanting to be helpful, I asked him what it was that he was worried about. His response was heartbreaking and insightful.

"Everything," he said. "I even worry that I worry too much." Oh, my sweet child! As a mother, of course, my natural response to him worrying so much was to worry about his worrying. This young man had always seemed so solid and grounded to me, and I immediately wanted to fix the problem for him. What was I going to do?

About this time, it occurred to me that I need to follow my own advice and listen to the wisdom I've come to through so much effort. Instead of pushing forward with how to solve the problem, I allowed myself to take a step back and assess it. As someone who understands how important it is to **Manage Your Own Stuff,** I had to make a bit of a leap to realize that this advice also applies to the young man I've been raising. Instead of managing his **stuff** for him, I suggested that he examine just what his **stuff** is. I asked him to write a list of all the things he was worried about.

INSTEAD OF MANAGING HIS STUFF FOR HIM, I SUGGESTED HE EXAMINE JUST WHAT HIS STUFF IS

Three full pages later, my son had written down all of his worries. Everything from "why do I bite my fingernails" to "will other people still like me" (Hey, that sounds a whole lot like worrying about what **They** think, doesn't it?) to "what am I going to do with my life." It's interesting to note that so many of the things we worry about phrase themselves in the form of a question. Worry isn't about dealing with a certain outcome, it's discomfort over not knowing what the outcome will be.

Writing out this enormous list of worries ended up being a helpful activity for my son. Seeing what **stuff** he had written made it much easier to figure out how to manage it. It's a lot like goal setting, in a sense, as it's nearly impossible to reach a goal if you haven't defined it. It's likewise difficult to seek solutions to what worries you without first recognizing what those things are. As soon as he had written his worries down, my son found that there were issues on the paper that he already knew how to fix. Rather than trying to manage his stuff for him, I gave him my unconditional love and support. As a result, naturally and without force, he loosened his grip on his own fears, anxieties, and worries. By my **holding space** for his quirks and colors, his own acceptance could take root. After all, who really cares if you bit your nails? It has absolutely nothing to do with the kind of person you are.

I have taken to heart a beautiful quote that is ascribed to Albert Einstein that basically says you can live everyday as if it is a miracle or live everyday as if it isn't. When we're constantly bogged down in worry, we're living in fear and as if nothing is a miracle, which often keeps us **Stuck in the Muck.** When I was worrying that my son was worrying about worrying, I told him, "Trees fall on people." We can't spend our lives fearful of everything that might or could happen.

Living authentically means allowing the world to be what it is, and even celebrating it. It's hard to trust a world where anything can happen, but to allow fear to keep you from celebrating life is a sure-fire way miss the millions of miracles that surround us every single day. Worrying removes the possibility of miracles from your awareness. Being caught up in the 'what if' takes us away from the moments.

All that we really have control over in a given moment is ourselves. We can strive to check our attitudes from moment to moment. The past is out of our control, as is the future. By maintaining authenticity, power, and **Grace,** we get the chance to experience the present—to allow **Magic in the Moment,** as we've already discussed.

We're often told that we have a choice of how we react every moment of every day. That is a powerful thought, but in and of itself, it can be intimidating. Every moment of every day? That sounds exhausting! Fortunately, when you get a handle on your worries you get the chance to let go of inhibitions and useless anxiety. It's not necessary to worry about how you're going to handle every moment of every day, rather just to focus on the one you're in. This is how we turn our worries into wisdom.

LOVE YOUR LABEL

AS I'VE SAID SO MANY TIMES, LIFE OFFERS THE RECOVERING ALPHAHOLIC MANY OPPORTUNITIES TO LEARN FROM OUR YOUNGERS. As a Recovering Alphaholic, I was so much less likely to notice the wisdom that sometimes exudes from those who haven't yet been convinced that there's only one right way to do something. A beautiful example of this played out for me with my youngest child.

Some time ago, my son went through the diagnostic process to determine if he has a learning disability. When all was said and done, the doctors bestowed upon him the label of ADHD (attention-deficit, hyperactivity disorder). This is a label that's been pretty common in our country. People continually share their theories about the cause of this disorder, often without regard as to the appropriateness of doing so. There are likewise plenty of people willing to share their opinions regarding the number of diagnoses, not to mention how they personally feel about treating ADHD with medication.

My son wasn't overly concerned with any of these things. His interest was in what exactly it was and how it would affect his life. As we were discussing the diagnosis, he wrote down **80HD.** Of course, my first instinct was to correct him and explain what each of the letters in the acronym stood for. Instead, I managed to take a moment,

ONCE WE UNDERSTAND BETTER, IT IS POSSIBLE TO COME FROM A PLACE OF LESS JUDGMENT

and in that time, the beauty of his thought process occurred to me. I saw how this "disability" actually allowed my son to think in a slightly different, and arguably more interesting way. I marveled at how creative his brain was. All of a sudden, the label ADHD meant something completely different than what we expected.

Once we understand something better, it is then possible to come from a place of far less judgment. In fact, we might even allow ourselves to be a little curious. When we look at something objectively, attempting to understand it from many different perspectives, we can learn to see the awesome—and far too often overlooked—gifts that come along with the labels we're given in life.

My son's diagnosis actually ended up teaching me about my own brain. I was able to recognize so much of myself in the diagnostic criteria. Realizing that I was also ADHD was jarring at first and felt negative, but just as I saw the gifts it brought to my son, I found similar gifts were given to me. Additionally, I began

I WAS ABLE TO EMBRACE THAT THIS LABEL HELPED MAKE ME MORE COLORFUL

to better understand some of my own patterns and beliefs and rather than submitting to shame, I was able to embrace that this label was something that helped define me and make me more colorful.

I began to give myself some of that all-important **Grace** for not having the ability to maintain laser-focus on a topic. I granted myself permission to accept it when I felt scattered or chaotic. Instead of beating myself up, I began to **love my label.** In fact, it brought a sense of relief. I felt as if my nature had been validated, and it brought about a feeling of inner peace where there had previously been turmoil.

Learning from my **Younger** in this way opened up my eyes to the futility of constantly comparing myself and my son to others, and even to my own ideal of what I "should" be. I felt that I had already taken great strides in managing my Multiple Sclerosis (another label I have come to embrace), but it was my son who taught me how to accept **80HD!**

Of course, this kind of acceptance doesn't usually happen overnight. I considered a variety of medications offered to me, for example, but chose to take a different path. I chose to focus on skills, not pills in order to incorporate ADHD into my life as more of a gift than a hindrance. It started as a true **Humbling Block,** with me resisting and resenting and feeling stupid. As I came to a place of acceptance, in no small part due to my son, I was able to see my ADHD as a **quirk;** and as I like to say, **Quirks Make You Colorful!**

Labels can be hard to accept. It often feels like someone is pointing a finger at you, as if you are to blame for some shortcoming about yourself. Perhaps worse yet, a label might cause you to point your own finger at this supposed flaw, to tell yourself that something isn't your fault because 'ADHD made me do it,' for example. And the next thing you know, you're pulling away from the station on the Victim Train. Being a passenger on this particular iron horse is terribly counterproductive for the **Recovering Alpha Female.** Heck, it's counterproductive for anyone. The best way to cut that ride short is to **Manage Your Own Stuff!** Not coincidentally, **Managing Your Own Stuff** is a whole lot easier when you happen to **Love Your Label.**

I'M WEIRD, AND SO ARE YOU

I USED TO BALK AT THE IDEA OF ANYONE CALLING ME WEIRD. I was an Alpha Female who knew how to get things done. You could call me innovative or unique or exceptional, but I was not comfortable with being weird. My, how things can change. Once I sought to operate from a **Place of Grace** and celebrate my **YOU-niqueness,** some of the things I did definitely fell into the category of "weird."

If I hadn't already realized it for myself, my kids were there to remind me. I strongly believe that **Woo-Woo is Not Coo-Coo,** but I absolutely admit that it can look pretty strange from the outside. In fact, one might even describe it as weird. I went from a life of rule-following and good impressions into one that led me outside during the full moon. I had feathers woven into my hair and burned incense to cleanse and started wearing turquoise stones for their ability to clear energy.

Being referred to as weird used to strike me as an insult. It meant that I wasn't living up to **expectations,** or doing things the way I "should." I was "wrong." At this point in life, however, the word is no longer derogatory. Negative connotations have gone by the wayside as I embrace what it means to be weird. When you're weird, it means that you don't conform. You don't contort your values or your own Knowing in order to fit into a prescribed box labeled Mom, Partner, Employee, Patient, etc. It turns out you can be all of those things

EMBRACE WHAT IT MEANS TO BE WEIRD

while still honoring your true self. Remember, when you embrace your **quirks,** they become your colors.

Really, this is another opportunity to **Love Your Label** or be **the Black Sheep.** It allows you to accept differences, most notably in and for yourself. Let's get one thing straight, though: We're all weird. Everyone wonders at some time or another if maybe they just aren't a little different than everyone else. The answer is a resounding "Yes!" So, if we're all weird, then why don't we embrace it? Why don't we all accept and celebrate our own colorful **quirks,** the things that make us **YOU-nique?**

We have a hard time accepting weird as good for the simple fact that we've spent a lifetime associating the word with something negative. After all, we put a fair amount of effort into making sure that other people don't see how weird we really are. The **Recovering Alphaholic** is so much less concerned with outside opinions and judgments, though. She is willing to take a personal inventory of the things she thinks make her weird and to consider that, just maybe, some of that weirdness is actually something else entirely.

THE THINGS WE CALL WEIRD ARE OFTEN SOME OF THE BEST THINGS ABOUT US

By definition, anything that is unusual can be considered weird. So, anything about you that is unusual could also be put into a category that we've ascribed negative connotations to. What the heck?! The things we call weird are often some of the best things about us. If you're unusually strong, unusually quirky, unusually insightful, unusually anything, then you're weird. But those are good things, right? We've learned to repress some of our most wonderful attributes for fear of being seen as weird.

Children are a beautiful model to follow when it comes to accepting that **I'm Weird and So Are You.** A child loves to discover they can do something unique or to excel at something others find difficult. "Mommy, look!" is basically a kid making sure that someone is witness to their incredible weirdness. I'd go so far as to say that in the lower elementary grades, telling someone they're weird is done in admiration more times than not. As we get older, we start to worry more about what **They** think of us, and being called weird is no longer a compliment.

My nonprofit, *Underground Kindness,* takes ideas such
as compassion and kindness to students, usually those in
high school. What I've found is that those kids are not
completely entrenched in society's view of what is weird.
They tend to have more flexible views, and it is amazing
to see the incredible **YOU-niqueness** that surfaces when
they are encouraged toward self-acceptance. Kids today are
seeking relief from the overdrive of life, and it is amazing
to witness what happens when someone **holds space**
and they are able to escape to a quiet, serene place within
themselves. Their small acts of resistance to the status quo
bring me incredible comfort, as it shows that the views of
the past don't necessarily have to carry over into the future.

I am willing to recognize that you might not be
interested in shouting all of your weirdness from the
rooftops, nor do I recommend it. The point isn't for
you to demand others to embrace your weirdness, the
point is for you to do it for yourself. Accepting and even
getting kind of excited about your quirks, colors, labels,
etc. is one of the most liberating things you can do
when learning to Live with Grace in mind and body.

If we reflect back on the first book, we can recall
asking "Who are **THEY,** anyway?" There's little point
in worrying if **They** think you're weird; because guess
what? **They** are weird, too. So, feel free to skip down
the street when others are walking. Go ahead and talk
to yourself. Heck, name your personalities if you'd like.
Get comfortable with the things that previously made

you uncomfortable, because that very well may be what makes you happy and colorful. And if someone gives you grief for it, confess it all. Just tell them **I'm Weird and So Are You.**

CANCEL THE COMPARATIVE NARRATIVE

I HAVE HEARD SO MANY PEOPLE COMPLAIN OF FEELING INADEQUATE AFTER SPENDING TIME ON SOCIAL MEDIA. You see parents who are clearly doing a better job than you, folks celebrating job promotions that you envy, or people having exciting adventures that you wish you could be on. Not only are we inundated with updates from people we know and admire, but it's all couched within a framework of advertising that is specifically designed to elicit feelings of lack and scarcity within us.

With effort, I managed to get myself out of the **Comparative Narrative.** While others see those status updates and family photos as a public record of their own lives, I just don't buy into it for myself. The idea that likes, clicks, and views are related to my self-worth…It just fills me with a whole lot of nope. Am I failing because I'm not vacationing in the Bahamas like so-and-so? Nope. Should I be embarrassed that even after watching that video tutorial, I still can't do a decent French braid? Nope.

Through the process of learning to **Live With Grace,** I've been able to replace the need for constant comparison with other, more authentic things. I strive for **Progress, Not Perfection,** and that makes me happy. I believe that **Quirks**

I STRIVE FOR PROGESS, NOT PERFECTION

Make You Colorful. When I say that I'm on the **Better-Than Plan,** the only person I'm trying to be better than is the one I was yesterday! In my case, I let go of social media to a very large degree, and it took a lot of that **Comparative Narrative** along with it.

That's not to say that the **Comparative Narrative** doesn't ever rear its ugly head. There are times when I run a tape in my head where I see myself never doing enough, never being enough—always needing to do more to validate my place in this world. Fortunately, I am usually able to recognize it for what it is. It was a great awareness when I discovered that this is a problem of epidemic proportions, to see that the results of living in the cycle of comparison are incredibly harsh.

The biggest problem with the **Comparative Narrative** is that it sets us up for failure at all times. Rather than celebrating ourselves and our **YOU-niqueness,** we constantly hold our accomplishments up against the milestones of others and look for our inadequacies. This leads to even more inner turmoil when our thoughts start to turn against those who we see as more successful than ourselves. We end up resenting others instead of feeling joy for their accomplishments and/ or resenting ourselves for not doing as well as they. Someone else's achievements are an opportunity to feel

SOMEONE ELSE'S ACHIEVEMENTS ARE AN OPPORTUNITY TO FEEL GRATITUDE ON THAT PERSON'S BEHALF AND TO SHARE IN THEIR SENSE OF PRIDE

gratitude on that person's behalf and to share in their sense of pride. Anger and resentment ruin what should be a happy, **quirky,** colorful moment in time.

I use social media as an example, because it's one that so many of us can relate to, but after assigning meaning and language to what I came to see as the **Comparative Narrative,** I realized it started long ago. Even as a child and adolescent, there was always a sense of competition in which I would judge myself as less-than. Whether it was interacting with boys, earning grades, or playing sports, I wanted to excel for reasons that didn't originate inside myself. I expended so much effort trying to be good enough that I didn't leave myself an opportunity to see that I already was.

That's not something that's unique to *my* youth, either. Our current education system is dripping with the

Comparative Narrative. We're constantly testing our children to determine if they're doing as well as their classmates. We go so far as to compare their supposed achievement against their contemporaries around the world, no less. To make sure they can compete on these tests, we have to make space in their schedules, which means there's less room for creativity. We tell children that if they need to solve a problem, it has to be done *precisely this way.* Art? Music? Critical thinking skills?

EXPECTATIONS ARE RESENTMENT IN THE MAKING

These all take a backseat to how a student compares to a set of predetermined **expectations.** And as we know, **Expectations are Resentment in the Making!** We've created a system of **Alpha-demics** in which we literally train our children to build lives that may one day leave them reading books like this one in an effort to recover.

We're all coming from our own place with varied histories and different talents. Making life into some sort of a competition doesn't honor any of those things about us. How much happier could we be if we chose to celebrate what we are rather than to lament what we are not? Being curious about things for the simple fact that they matter to you and not because you want to emulate someone else—that's authenticity. Turning that curiosity into discovery—that is the nobility of purpose.

It's likely that none of us will ever be the prettiest/most talented/wealthiest/most active/healthiest person in the world. (Or the town. Possibly even the neighborhood.) Is being the prettiest/most talented/wealthiest/most active/healthiest really the point of life, though? When you live with self-acceptance and choose a **walk of Grace,** you find that you are already as _____ as you need to be, and that is enough. Just being you is **YOU-nique** and colorful! The **Comparative Narrative** fades away as you start to practice this journey of self acceptance.

GET CERTAIN WITH UNCERTAINTY

FOR MOST OF MY LIFE, ANY FEELINGS OF UNCERTAINTY REGISTERED TO ME ALMOST LIKE EMERGENCIES. Being unsure about a situation or an outcome wasn't a reality to accept, rather it was a problem that needed to be solved. Of course, striving to quell any uncertainty that happens to pop up in life is just asking for disappointment and frustration since even an Alpha Female simply can't control everything. Uncertainty would lead me to worry, and worrying just takes you right out of the moment and out of your state of being - typically throwing us into the **Frenetic Energetic** and **Alpha Overdrive.**

WORRYING RARELY HELPS AND DOESN'T SOLVE PROBLEMS

And guess what? Worrying rarely actually helps. It doesn't solve problems. In fact, it creates more... It can cause self doubt, and often insecurities and fear will come bubbling up. It even affects us physically as migraines, autoimmune flare ups, or depression, just to name a few possibilities.

It took a special effort on my part, but I have come to a place now where I not only accept uncertainty in my life, but **HOLD SPACE** for it to grow. That's quite a departure from the controlling personality I used to have, but it's been a

I LIKE TO VISUALIZE UNCERTAINTY AND ITS CHARACTERISTICS AS A BEAUTIFUL FLOWER

liberating and transformative experience that I encourage you try. Start slowly, and you may ultimately find that you are able to embrace uncertainty.

I like to visualize uncertainty and its characteristics (both the scary ones and the empowering ones) as a beautiful flower. In the center of that flower are those beautiful ideals we **RAFs** are striving to allow into our own lives: Things like trusting our journey and belief in oneself. There is an ease and a **flow** in that and a feeling of being **Zentered.** Keep in mind, too, that the center of the flower is where the seeds are formed.

The petals of the flower are the showy parts, though, aren't they? The color, the fragrance, the physical beauty…Whether you're talking about your flower or someone else's, your opinion is often based on how you judge the appearance of those petals. The center is where the seeds are formed, and the roots nourish the plant, but it's the petals that get all the attention. They also tend to represent our areas of uncertainty and the accompanying fear. Basically, that means that the things we most harshly judge ourselves on and use to determine our value are often the very things we can least control!

And where are the areas that we feel most uncertain? What are the things we most want to control and are least able? Most of my biggest uncertainties are shown in the diagram below. Maybe yours are similar, or maybe they're different. Either way, use this visual as a starting point to picture your own areas of uncertainty.

LET UNCERTAINTY GROW

Maybe, like mine, so much uncertainty played out in relationships. Growing up in a Catholic family, I had an understanding of how romantic relationships were meant to look. It starts with dating, leads to marriage, kids and family...

Except it doesn't necessarily have to. I have now been in a relationship with my Sweetheart for more than twelve years, and it has been an important part of learning to **Let Uncertainty Grow.** I have learned to recognize that our relationship is wonderful "right now," and I am so very happy when I can relish in that. We both win. In my Alpha days, I would have to push to make sure my **expectations** for the progression of a relationship were met; and I likely would have pushed my sweetheart away and missed out on this incredible decade with him.

This was pivotal in me getting comfortable accepting the uncertainty of life. I remember at one point when he was closing down, I made the very raw and genuine comment that "If you didn't want to be with me, please go as I want you to be happy." It was risky and scary for me to offer but it came from a total **Place of Grace** - unbeknownst to me it took pressure off the 'right relationship/fairytale' future he was feeling bottlenecked by.

Parenting is another petal of my flower of uncertainty. As parents, we tend to want things to be better for our children than they were for us, and we want to be the ones who make it happen. We want their lives to be a little easier, for them to have a little more, for them to be a little healthier. Don't forget, either, that those petals are what the outside world tends to judge us on, so in addition to wanting to do things right for my kids, I was also letting everyone else's **expectations** inform my choices. "No, you can't wear that shirt to church. What would Grandma think?" Instead of cultivating an authentic accepting relationship with my children, I would try to plan, control and manage their **stuff.** In this process, I would unknowingly usurp their trust in themselves by pushing an agenda that I thought was right for them. In the name of "giving them a better life" I would disempower them and plant their own seeds of uncertainty. Hello, Paradox!

Whether we're talking about finances, professional development, or even my health, all of these fears needed to fall away to regain my trust in myself. I needed to let uncertainty bloom and grow. When you start to find the ease around uncertainty, amazing things start to happen. For example, the question "What's next?" starts to take on a whole new life. When you're working from fear of uncertainty, "What's next?" is an exasperated and frightful accusation. When you accept uncertainty, however, "What's next?" becomes a doorway. It's not dread, but curiosity that leads us to ask that question. Uncertainty begins to look like possibilities and opportunities.

In order for the center of the flower to bear its seeds, each of the petals has to fade and eventually fall. That's pretty scary at first, but when you look closer, you realize that what it really represents is liberation, freedom, and non-attachment. It represents trust and letting go. One surprising outcome is that you tend to find that accepting the uncertainty is actually so much easier and

"WHAT'S NEXT?" CAN BECOME A DOORWAY TO NEW POSSIBILITIES AND OPPORTUNITIES

more fruitful than fighting against it ever was. You start to wonder why you wasted so much time being fearful and attempting to control that which can't be controlled. As I said before "trees fall on people."

FLUIDITY NOT RIGIDITY

AS RECOVERING ALPHA FEMALES WE ARE IN THE PROCESS OF SOFTENING AND ALLOWING OURSELVES TO BE COMFORTABLE AND AT EASE. As a result, we are constantly moving, transitioning, and adjusting. This requires us to embrace fluidity and release rigidity. This movement is reflective instead of reactive. It is important that we tune in to this omega energy so that we may learn to soften and reach a state of **flow.** In addition to encouraging our own **flow,** incorporating fluidity also brings us the capacity to **hold space** for others so they may also make adjustments as they are in their own flux.

We've talked before about the feeling of being in **flow.** It's when your creativity or passion comes forth authentically. It takes micro adjustments to reach a state of **flow.** For example, we may change our outfit a couple of times, amend our coffee order, or reschedule a meeting for convenience. This process is one of fluidity, and should not be mistaken with being flaky or indecisive.

As you start to live more in **flow** you will honor your body and continue learning to trust its notions.

Just like in the airplane, you need to put your own oxygen mask on first so you can then inspire others find their own safety and security. Your ability to be fluid rather than rigid creates a ripple effect. It encourages kinship and general respect and understanding for the needs of others as they make their own adjustments. Rigidity is such a **flow** stopper because it allows no room for creative expression. It doesn't allow you to morph and transition into your truest, most authentic self.

Sometimes being fluid can look a lot like being ambivalent or even flaky, however the title of 'ambivalent' is something sourced from **Them,** rather than being a true representation of who you are. In your life, **They** might be a congregation of PTA ladies who drain your energy, an in-law who undermines you, or even a "friend" who can't quite understand your new practice of unconditional acceptance. Know that as you practice the movement away from rigidity and toward fluidity, your opinion is the only one that matters. Others' approval may be externally flattering, but self acceptance is imperative. Accepting your own needs, in turn, provides a strong basis to accept that others have their own **YOU-nique** expressions.. It's all about navigating the best that you can with your instinct as your guide while creating the most graceful, authentic journey as possible.

Holding space for yourself allows you to walk a little lighter, but it requires you to navigate your own needs. A powerful means for doing this is to focus on **Fluidity Not Rigidity,** which requires making adjustments. Doing so is integral to your own development and does not automatically mean you are flaky or indecisive. It means you have read the situation, recognized your needs, and recalibrated when necessary. Practice non-judgment for yourself and others. Practice unconditional acceptance and loving the light that you are, and disregard how others might perceive that love.

BE YOUR OWN WOO-WOO GURU

THE AMAZING THING ABOUT MY JOURNEY AS A RECOVERING ALPHAHOLIC IS THAT IT HAS LED ME TO SO MANY WOO-WOO GURUS WHO HAVE BEEN ESSENTIAL TO HELPING ME FIND UNDERSTANDING. However, as I become wiser and start to love and trust myself more I have also developed a strong sense of gratitude for my own abilities. I am so blessed and grateful for all the versions of myself that I have journeyed with and developed.

In the first book the **Recovering Alpha Female** is given the tools to start trusting her own intuition, which will eventually be the only tool she needs. If we gain the strength and ability to trust our intuition, our gut feelings, we may then move into **Grace.** Would you like to know a little secret? **Grace** is actually the way that we use these tools. As a **Recovering Alpha Female** I am making progress in gaining both strength and **Grace.** To be strong yet soft.

The first step toward becoming my own **Woo-Woo Guru** is getting to know my **Knowing.** This means getting **Zentered,** getting quiet, and settling into a place where I am in touch with my core self. This is one reason that I have taken up the practice of yoga, because it encourages me to trust myself and to rely on my core. When I am in this quiet zone of self-acceptance, I am more aware of my own intuition. I am more trusting that I will make the kindest, most gracious decisions for my body and for those around me. A practical example of this would be my eating habits. If I am busy and noisy running around from meeting to meeting then I might quickly chow down whatever is in sight. Due to my Multiple Sclerosis, this eating habit would be very unkind to my own health and wellness.

FLUIDITY RIPPLES OUT AND ENCOURAGES UNDERSTANDING AND RESPECT FOR THE UNIQUE FLOW OF OTHERS

In addition, if one of my kiddos is witnessing my poor eating habit then they aren't receiving a good example of health and self-love. On the other hand, if I get quiet and feel loving towards my body then I am more likely to see the wisdom of canceling one of my appointments, and maybe even inviting my family over to a good meal served at the dining room table. In this scenario there would be healthy, home cooked food eaten around a table with loved ones and enough time to digest before doing something else.

As we get to know our **Knowing** and trust our intuition, we may feel more comfortable doing what is necessary to feel good and stable and graceful in our lives. Unsurprisingly, an important factor of this is **Holding Space** for yourself. This could include time that you set aside for yourself in a moment that could otherwise go sour. When we take time to walk a little softer and to judge ourselves a little less harshly, we are holding that space that is so necessary to make a better decision or to choose kindness over mental hardness. As I **hold space** for myself, I find that I am more aware and accepting of my own actions. I see my flaws and remind them that they are my colors. As a result, I am more accepting of other's actions, too. I see that other people are not flawed, but simply a beautiful combination of colors.

When I am my kindest self, I see myself in Christ's image. I see myself as someone who is doing the best with what she has to make the world a more graceful place. I view myself with more self-love and engage in less self-bullying. I begin to see myself as somebody that I can look up to and take advice from. I see myself becoming my own **Woo-Woo Guru.** Although I do have Bambi legs sometimes, I feel more confident with my walk on this earth. I feel lighter and more graceful. I have come to feel that I am no longer a burden to myself, but rather a joyous companion that I have been blessed enough to journey with.

Epilogue: Living in Grace

ACCEPTING THE JOURNEY

ONE OF THE BEAUTIFUL CHARACTER TRAITS OF AN ALPHA FEMALE IS THAT WE WILL, IN FACT, PUT OURSELVES "OUT THERE." It often doesn't matter if we have specific training or education or even financial means. We figure out a way to make it happen!

This way definitely underscores the principles of courage described earlier in this book. Just because it is courageous, however, doesn't mean it's the most efficient. The path of the **Recovering Alpha Female** movement has been a somewhat winding one, with each detour leading to discoveries and understandings that furthered the **RAF** story. In fact, The **Recovering Alpha Female** was one of my earliest creations. The self-acceptance I experienced was something I truly wanted to share with other women.

That awakening also called me to humble myself in a big way. What followed was the creation of

Underground Kindness. This nonprofit organization was developed as a type of wellness curriculum that has been implemented in schools for the purpose of holding space for our **Youngers.** Throughout the various stages of that project, I have continued to circle back to the **Recovering Alpha Female** cause.

AFTER "LAUNCH" AND "LEARN" COMES "LIVE"

I incubated the nonprofit and wrote my first book… neither with much experience or formal training. (Because that's what we Alphas do, right?) I have launched my projects and I have learned from them. One of the lessons that I work to internalize is that after "launch" and "learn" comes "live." As a **Recovering Alpha Female** I have the fortitude to step back from these enormous projects and live a life separate from their creation.

I have come to realize that both *Underground Kindness* and the **Recovering Alpha Female** are a part of a movement that strives to bring **Grace** and self acceptance. We all know by now that when an Alpha gets on task, she can quickly become too serious and work herself into a frenetic energetic where she wants to offer force instead of **Grace,** again, driven by the external which throws your body back into **Alpha Overdrive.** This is a warning sign to myself and to the other **RAFs** out there to step into **Grace** and soften. These projects that are my greatest joy are not allowed to be the reason I get **Stuck in the Muck.** Instead, they are opportunities to **choose my checklist**--filling it with highlighters and happy pens-- and to thoroughly appreciate small moments with family and friends.

It has taken me years of work and dedication to launch my contribution to the planet. I have learned so much about the importance of connections and single moments in time. I am awake and called, and I will remember to celebrate my **quirks** and **hold space** through transformation and remember, **Progress, Not Perfection.**

As you come to the close of the second book in this series, I ask that you choose to reflect rather than react. Some of the things discussed in these pages might touch a raw nerve for you. "Get certain about uncertainty? Who's she kidding?" "My **quirks** aren't the cute kind!" "Chakras? Seriously?" I don't expect that everything I have to say will resonate for you. Some of it might leave you empowered, while other things leave you feeling rather defensive or offended. It's those tidbits that cause you to really react, however, that provide you a little extra incentive to look deeper. I've said repeatedly that you don't need to get too bogged down asking yourself Why? over and over, but should you find that something causes strong feelings in you, use it as a catalyst for reflection. Challenge yourself to step out of the muck, to try something new, to be kinder, gentler, and more authentic with yourself. Because it is in keeping an open mind and an open heart that we can find **Grace.**

LEARN MORE ABOUT LINDY'S VISION OF UNCONDITIONAL ACCEPTANCE

LET YOUR COLOR OUT:

The **Walk of Grace** is not an easy Journey to embark on. It is full of **humbling blocks,** tears, transformations, and ah-ha moments. **Let Your Color Out** is designed to guide and encourage women as they step into this walk. **LYCO** supports over-achieving women as they begin to **choose the checklist,** take time to get quiet, walk a little softer, and embrace their colorful **quirks.** Guidance is offered through the **Recovering Alpha Female** book series as well as **Your Health is Your Wealth** and speaking engagements. This company inspires unconditional self-acceptance in women and encourages them to **hold space** for transformation while stepping fully into an authentic, colorful life. **www.lindylewis.com**

Lindy's Vision of Unconditional Acceptance Starts with our Youngers:

Underground Kindness is a non-profit organization that introduces young people to the practice and philosophies of stress reduction and mindful living as they practice unconditional acceptance of self and others.

Underground Kindness creates a learning environment that is free of judgement, **expectation** and competition. It is our vision to encourage and nurture through all-inclusive classroom programs such as; Self-Bullying, Stress Management, Authentic Relating, Creative Journaling, Relationship 101, Yoga, Meditation, Being Younique, and Team Building.

Our goal is to provide classes and workshops that support the growth of our **Youngers** into self-reflective, expressive, happy, authentic, members of society. Students are given tools, tips, and techniques to manage their own **stuff** while giving unconditional acceptance to others. The safe environment that they are offered allows our **Youngers** to practice inter-personal skills and compassion for self and others so to ripple that back out into their world.

Inspiring Students, Supporting Teachers, and Connecting Community

All Underground Kindness classes are FREE to students and the schools!
We are supported 100% by the generosity of grants and donations.

KINDNESS IS CONTAGIOUS...
For more information please visit:
www.undergroundkindness.org

Printed in the United States
By Bookmasters